Service-Learning — Guide & Journal
Higher Education Edition
Robert Max Schoenfeld

Special Thank You to the Following Service-Learning Professionals for Their Advice and Assistance:

Lyvier Conss	Campus Compact – Community Colleges
Janet Griffin	Howard University
Terry Pickeral	National Center for Learning and Citizenship
Seth Pollack	California State University – Monterey Bay
Gail Robinson	American Association of Community Colleges
Daniel Stallings	Ball State University
Carla Turner	Colorado State University
Nicole Vessell	California State University – Northridge
Laurie Worral	DePaul University
Josh Young	Miami Dade Community College

ISBN: 0-9744504-3-X

Graphic Design: Taeyeun Kim and Andrew Schlotfeldt

Additional copies may be ordered from:
Guide & Journal Publications
5235 South Graham Street
Seattle, WA 98118
E-mail: Info@ServiceLearningHigherEd.com
www.ServiceLearningHigherEd.com
Fax: 206-721-3200

Additional Titles by the Author:
Service-Learning — Student's Guide & Journal for Middle & High School
Service-Learning — Student's Guide & Journal for Elementary School

CONTENTS

SERVICE-LEARNING — A DEFINITION

Service-Learning is a method of teaching and learning that enriches your academic life and life-long learning by engaging you in meaningful hands-on service to the community while gaining valuable knowledge and skills that integrate with course objectives. Service-Learning focuses on critical reflective thinking and experiential learning that address local needs and foster civic responsibility.

CREATING A BETTER FUTURE

SERVICE-LEARNING offers you the opportunity to take charge of your future:

- ❖ Clarify your personal values while pursuing your academic studies.

- ❖ Gain a sense of personal inner satisfaction that comes from doing something meaningful for others.

- ❖ Identify and research a need within your community and evaluate ways to fulfill that need.

- ❖ Participate in socially responsible activities that will have a positive impact not only on your community but also on the nation and the world.

- ❖ Gain experience about the world in a dynamic and interactive way.

- ❖ Gain knowledge and insights that will prepare you for active civic engagement.

- ❖ Reflect on how to maximize your personal and academic development to help you achieve your goals in life.

- ❖ Acquire skills that are transferable to your future work environments.

SERVICE-LEARNING — KEY COMPONENTS

**There are six key components of Service-Learning:
(1) Connecting Service with Learning, (2) Reflection,
(3) Reciprocity, (4) Critical Thinking, (5) Social Responsibility,
and (6) Experiential Learning.**

Connecting Service with Learning

A successful Service-Learning project must include meaningful service and be academically rigorous. High-level Service-Learning is achieved when the student is actively engaged in community service that has a significant positive impact on everyone involved – the student, the instructor, the community service provider, and the people within the community. In addition, the student must meet or exceed the academic objectives stated by the instructor and/or specified in the course syllabus. (In most Service-Learning programs the student is evaluated on the course work and knowledge gained and not merely on the service performed.)

Reflection

Service-Learning Reflection includes the following activities by the student:

- Assess personal interests, knowledge, skills, and attributes that will be useful in performing the Service-Learning project.
- Stand back and make a fresh and comprehensive assessment of specific needs in the community.
- Reflect on how to effectively participate in the community to meet the identified need(s).
- Evaluate the progress of the project and fine-tune actions to best reach the desired outcome.
- Reflect, at the conclusion of the project, on personal changes and changes to others within the community (e.g., knowledge gained, skills acquired, changes in perception, personal growth, and connection to the community).

Reciprocity

Service-Learning is a vehicle that makes it possible for the student to both give and receive. The student offers time, energy, knowledge, and creativity to address a specific need in the community and in return receives professional advice and direction from community service providers, mentors, and faculty. Thus, in addition to the education received as part of academic activities, the student receives real-life knowledge and gains a sense of empathy, connection, and mission from the people with whom he or she is serving and working.

Critical Thinking

Service-Learning places the student in situations that facilitate reflective and analytical thinking, as well as the development of creative and effective problem-solving skills.

Social Responsibility

Many Service-Learning projects place the student into a multicultural environment that expands the student's compassion, civic awareness, and desire to be civically engaged.

Experiential Learning

Service-Learning uses direct experience and hands-on learning to help the student learn to take initiative, assume responsibility, and become self-sufficient as well as improve deliberative, collaborative, and leadership skills. The Service-Learning experience helps the student grow in knowledge, skills, and awareness that will prove useful in future career(s), in family life, and in involvement in the community.

SERVICE-LEARNING — A HISTORY

Service-Learning traces its inception back to the administration of Abraham Lincoln. In 1864, the Morrill & Homestead Initiatives created land grants to establish colleges throughout the nation that focused on creating "citizens who are educated for the betterment of society." Leland Stanford, founder of Stanford University, addressed this issue at the inauguration of the university on November 11, 1885, when he stated, "The objectives of the university are to qualify students for personal success and direct usefulness in life and to promote the public welfare by exercising an influence on behalf of humanity and civilization." Since that time, the mission statement of most colleges and universities has included the concept of student development through the transfer of knowledge and active public service to advance civilization.

Almost 20 years later, in 1903, the University of Cincinnati created the Cooperative Education Movement that let students combine learning, service, and career. Later in the century, progressive thinkers John Dewey and William James became the first to incorporate experiential learning and service to the community into the educational system.

In the early to mid 20th century came the establishment of voluntary associations that focused on service in the community (e.g., YMCA/YWCA and Rotary) and government agencies (e.g., Civilian Conservation Corps and National Youth Administration). In the 1960s, President Kennedy gave a call to service that led to development of the Peace Corps and Vista.

In 1985, Campus Compact was founded by the presidents of Stanford, Brown, and Georgetown Universities and by the presidents of the Education Commission of the States to help establish and support Service-Learning on campuses across the nation. There are currently more than 900 colleges and universities with Campus Compact offices. Campus Compact offers a vast array of resources that help to facilitate the development of student citizenship skills and values, encourage partnerships between campus and community, support faculty, and encourage research. The Campus Compact Website has information about collegiate Service-Learning and lists the dates and locations of national and regional Service-Learning conferences. (The Campus Compact Website is: www.compact.org)

Today, in the United States, there are more than four million students who are donating their time and their expertise to Service-Learning projects. Think of it – you are participating in one of the most powerful programs for change in the world. And you will be joining millions of your peers to create a better future for this nation and for the world.

GETTING STARTED

There are two avenues for Service-Learning: Faculty-Directed Service-Learning and Student-Directed Service Learning.

❖ **Faculty-Directed Service-Learning** — The instructor either assigns a Service-Learning project to the student or provides the student with a list of Service-Learning projects from which to choose. The instructor oversees the student and monitors the project's progress to make sure it meets the academic requirements for the class.

❖ **Student-Directed Service-Learning** — The student identifies and researches a specific need in the community and develops a Service-Learning project that addresses that need. The instructor oversees the student and monitors the project's progress to make sure it meets the academic requirements for the class.

FACULTY-DIRECTED SERVICE-LEARNING

❖ Review syllabus to identify academic course objectives.
❖ Meet with your instructor to ensure you understand the assignment and the learning objectives.
❖ Identify personal learning goals and areas of interest for service.
❖ Meet with community service provider for orientation.

- ❖ Draft a Plan of Action (refer to page 17).
- ❖ Complete required training and screening requirements, as determined and arranged by your instructor and the community service provider.
- ❖ Make the time commitment and commence service experience.
- ❖ Complete periodic service logs, reflections, and assignments (pages 18–47).

STUDENT-DIRECTED SERVICE-LEARNING

CREATING A SERVICE-LEARNING PROJECT

- ❖ Review syllabus to identify academic course objectives.
- ❖ Meet with your instructor to ensure you understand the assignment and the learning objectives.
- ❖ Identify a Service-Learning project that you find meaningful, that ties in with your course objectives, and that uses your knowledge, experience, and skills. You can carry out a Service-Learning project as an individual or you can assemble a team of students, including students from other colleges and universities. (The instructor must approve your Service-Learning project.)
- ❖ Conduct research on the needs in your community by using the Internet (see page 51), by contacting social service agencies (e.g., The United Way, religious organizations, food banks, and environmental organizations), or by making personal observations or using personal networks and connections.
- ❖ Meet with your instructor to draft a Plan of Action (refer to page 17). A Plan of Action must include a paragraph on each of the following areas:
  - ❖ Project mission statement.
  - ❖ Step-by-step plan to fulfill the project's mission.
  - ❖ Vision of the project's end goal – impact on the community, the college/university, the people served, the community service agency, and on you.
  - ❖ Ways in which the Service-Learning project will enhance your academic studies.
- ❖ Make the time commitment and commence service experience.
- ❖ Complete periodic service logs, reflections, and assignments (pages 18–47).

(Note: There is only so much that can be accomplished in one quarter or semester. To make a meaningful and lasting change in your community and gain the full benefits that Service-Learning has to offer, you may want to enroll in several Service-Learning classes during your college/university education.)

COMMITMENT TO THE SERVICE-LEARNING PROJECT

_____

*Signature**

_____

Date

*By signing, I am making the commitment to perform and complete
a Service-Learning project that will have a positive impact on myself and the community
and meet the course's academic requirements.

SOLVING PROBLEMS AT THEIR SOURCE

Your Service-Learning project will address an issue or problem within the community. Research and evaluate the source of the problem (e.g., homelessness, hunger, illiteracy, environmental destruction, disease, crime, domestic violence, teenage antisocial behavior) on the local and national levels. Reflect on how your Service-Learning project will make a lasting and positive impact that makes progress toward resolution of the problem.

VISIONARY PLANNING

Take responsibility for your future – take action in your community that will lead to the creation of a dynamic, healthy, clean, generous, and prosperous society. Reflect on how you can make a sustainable change. Create a farsighted vision for your future and the future of your community and create a Plan of Action to make it a reality.

LIVING A SUCCESSFUL LIFE

A successful person is one whose actions are founded on inner wisdom and personal character. A person of high character shows traits of caring for the welfare of others, honesty, fairness, responsibility, and respect for others and self. You will cultivate success by infusing your life with enthusiasm, integrity, creativity, vision, generosity, appreciation, and wisdom.

GAINING WISDOM

Wisdom is inner knowledge that will help you discern correct thought and action that leads to happiness and success in life. Wisdom comes from quiet reflection, from being in the company of a person with experience (mentor), and from assessing life's experiences.

Action combined with Wisdom gives you Power—
Power to create a better future for you and your community.

FINDING A MENTOR

Seek out someone you respect and aspire to emulate. Ask him or her to mentor you in specific areas so you can acquire the knowledge and skills you need to make your Service-Learning project a success.

A mentor can be a valuable advisor who can assist you throughout all stages of your project, helping you:

- Develop a Plan of Action.
- Implement your project.
- Identify and contact professionals and specialists who have knowledge or expertise that is relevant to your project.
- Solve problems.
- Reflect on the meaning and potential impact of your project.

BE A SERVICE-LEARNING LIFE COACH

(This may be optional—ask your instructor)

A Service-Learning Life Coach is a guide and mentor who provides knowledge, skills, and wisdom that help a younger student acquire the tools he or she needs to live a successful life. A Service-Learning Life Coach is a friend who shares one hour per week (or more) assisting with such activities as reading, writing, arithmetic, learning a new sport, and guiding the mentee. A Service-Learning Life Coach is one who exhibits the highest level of integrity and whose actions are in the best interests of the mentee.

SERVICE-LEARNING LIFE COACH AGREEMENT

I,_____ , will be a Service-Learning Life Coach to
(Your Name)

_____ because I want him/her to live a successful life.
(Student Name)

I agree to spend one hour (or more) per week helping with schoolwork,

teaching new skills or sports, answering questions, and sharing my knowledge

and wisdom in ways that will empower_____ to be
(Student Name)

the best that he/she can be.

I agree to be a Life Coach for_____ for one academic
(Student Name)

year. This agreement can be renewed every year.

_____
(Life Coach Signature)

_____
(Date)

EXAMPLES OF SERVICE-LEARNING PROJECTS

Following are a number of ideas in a variety of areas to help stimulate your thinking and planning for your Service-Learning project.

Architecture

Once a month bring together youth from the inner city. Brainstorm with them about specific ways to improve the livability of their community. Draw up a plan to improve parks, schools, homes, and office buildings. Help the students put together a scale model of the plan. Have the students present their plan to the mayor and the city council.

Agriculture

Today many Americans have accumulations of chemical pesticides, herbicides, and fertilizers in their bodies, and many of these chemicals are known to cause diseases such as cancer. Develop a plan that will help persuade farmers to use sustainable agriculture techniques that minimize the use of chemicals. Work with farmers and government officials in your community to implement your plan. Share your plan with students in agriculture schools across the nation and help them replicate your success. You can learn more about this subject by searching the Web for "sustainable agriculture."

Art

Scientists have found that specific colors facilitate emotional and physical healing. Develop an art program at the local children's hospital using proven techniques of art therapy. Introduce your program to the administrators of your local hospitals and help them implement your program. Share your program with college and university students across the nation and help them establish similar programs in hospitals in their own communities. You can learn more about this subject by searching the Web for "art therapy."

Business & Economics

Identify government and private policies that lead to poverty, homelessness, and unemployment in your community. Develop and implement an economic plan that will help lift people in your community out of poverty. Help students in colleges and universities across the nation develop and institutionalize similar programs in their own communities. You can learn more about this subject by searching the Web for "poverty," "homelessness," and "unemployment."

Computer Science

Show elementary school students how to create a website. Help the students build a website that includes pictures and that describes the Service-Learning projects in which the elementary students have participated. Help the students create a national Service-Learning network on their website that makes it possible for students from different geographic areas to share ideas with each other.

Education & English

Organize a "Study Buddy" Program in which older students tutor and mentor younger students one-on-one in reading, spelling, or math. For example, once a week for a school year, have sixth grade students tutor second grade students in reading skills. Put a plan in motion that helps the "Study Buddy" Program continue year after year.

Math

Bring math to life with one-on-one mentoring. Develop and implement a math mentoring program in which math students from your college/university meet one-on-one with students from an elementary, middle, or high school. Develop a matrix that allows the math department at the university to track the progress of the mentored students. On a yearly basis (starting with first grade through high school), compare the tutored student's math test scores and attitudes about math with the test scores and attitudes about math of students of the same age and in the same school who did not take part in the program. Institutionalize the program and help colleges and universities across the United States develop similar programs.

Medicine & Health

Identify and research ways to improve the health of youth in your community by persuading them to make changes in their life-styles (e.g., improving their diets, stopping smoking, and increasing exercise). Develop a Plan of Action that includes specific activities to reduce the risk of diseases such as diabetes, obesity, heart disease, hypertension, and cancer. Introduce your Plan of Action to the local school board, PTA, YMCA, and/or other youth advocacy associations and help them implement a five-year plan that includes a mechanism for annual evaluations.

Philosophy

Involve at-risk kids in activities to clean up their community. Talk with the kids about their beliefs on life and how they can take steps to create a positive and healthy future for themselves. Identify Life Coaches for all of the kids (one for each kid) who will help them create and implement a life plan that guides them in achieving a fulfilling and productive life.

Political Science, History, Communications, Speech, & Civics

Teach elementary, middle, or high school students how to make positive and conflict-free changes in their lives by way of speaking, writing, voting, peaceful assembly, and lobbying. Give each student a copy of the Declaration of Independence, the Constitution, and the Bill of Rights, and have them take turns reading excerpts from the documents to the class. Help each student compose five action steps that will help him or her bring about positive change in his or her personal life, in the school, and in the community. Reflect with the students about how they can implement their action steps.

Science & Environmental Studies

Evaluate the quality of the drinking water in your community and develop a plan to reduce or eliminate pollutants in the water. Work with your local water board and city or other officials to put your plan into action. Share your plan with students at colleges/universities across the nation and help them replicate your success in their own communities.

Sociology

Develop a questionnaire that asks students why they do or do not get involved with volunteering in their community, and use it to interview 100 students on your campus. Evaluate your findings and develop a plan that will motivate more students to volunteer. Present your plan to the director of the volunteer center on campus and help implement the plan.

Women's Studies

Help improve the lives of single mothers and their children. Research the economic, social, and physical needs of single mothers in your community. Develop and implement a plan that improves their financial, physical, and emotional well-being. Work with local and national organizations such as the YWCA, National Organization for Women, and the Casey Foundation to implement your program on a local and a national basis.

INTERDISCIPLINARY SERVICE-LEARNING PROJECTS
Working in Partnership with Other Students to Fulfill the Mission of Your Service-Learning Project

Reducing Pollution

Fifty-five percent of the nation's air pollution and much of the water pollution comes from our use of petroleum-powered transportation. Now is the time to replace this century-old technology with vehicles that produce no or only minute amounts of pollution. Assemble a Service-Learning team that includes not only students who are working on the design and development of green cars, but also students who are studying mechanical engineering, chemical engineering, auto mechanics, computer science, physics, environmental sciences, art, design, business, and marketing. Work with automotive manufacturers and environmental organizations to develop and implement a plan for the production and sale of a state-of-the-art green vehicle. You can learn more about this subject at www.nesea.org and www.greenercars.com, and by searching the Web for "green car."

Reducing Crime

Today there are more than two million citizens in America's prisons. Research the social, economic, and political causes of crime and sentencing guidelines. Work with students from sociology, law, law enforcement, economics, business, women's studies, and political science to develop and implement a plan that reduces crime in your community. Take your findings to the civic and political leaders in your community and to the United States Attorney General, and work with them to bring your plan to the entire country.

Getting Young Americans Involved in Our Democracy

A healthy democracy requires that the nation's citizens participate in the democratic process. In the 2000 presidential election less than 36% of citizens 18 to 25 years old took the time to vote. Working with students from political science, law, history, philosophy, sociology, business, and marketing develop and implement a plan that gets young people involved in civic activities, making them active participants in voting, campaigning, and running for office. Work with civic and political leaders and the offices of the Secretary of State (in each state) to put your plan in place locally and across the nation.

Creating a More Peaceful World

International and civil conflicts persist despite the efforts of political leaders, international associations (e.g., United Nations), and peace-loving citizens. Assemble an international team of students who are involved in international studies, environmental science, economics, sociology, history, law, communication, agriculture, international finance, women's studies, and conflict resolution. Develop a Plan of Action that reduces the stresses that cause conflict locally, nationally, and internationally. Engage your international team in implementing your Plan of Action in communities throughout the world.

Create a National and International Service-Learning Team

Work in partnership with students in other disciplines at your university and with students in universities across the United States and internationally to resolve major problems in our communities, the nation, and throughout the world.

Set up a website and a list-serve to facilitate communication with the students on your team. Have your team meet annually at one of the national Service-Learning conferences.

Numerous grants are available to help you fund your project.
Please go to: **www.compact.org/grants**

SERVICE-LEARNING PROJECT

Title: _____

Course Title: _____ **Course Number:** _____

Service-Learning Project Mission Statement: _____

_____

_____

_____

_____

I Intend to Learn: _____

_____

_____

_____

I Intend to Accomplish: _____

_____

_____

_____

This Ties in to Course Goals/Objectives in the Following Ways: _____

_____

_____

_____

_____

RESEARCHING THE PROBLEM

The following sources were valuable in gaining the knowledge I needed to understand
the problem and to take the action necessary to make a lasting positive change.
(books, periodicals, interviews, websites, and assigned material)

Source #1: _____

                   Title   Author   Date

Synopsis of my findings: _____

_____

_____

_____

_____

Issues for Follow-Up Investigation: _____

_____

_____

Source #2: _____

                   Title   Author   Date

Synopsis of my findings: _____

_____

_____

_____

_____

Issues for Follow-Up Investigation: _____

_____

_____

Source #3: _____
　　　　　　　　　　　Title　　　　　　　　　　　　　　　Author　　　　　　　　　Date

Synopsis of my findings: _____

_____

_____

_____

_____

_____

_____

Issues for Follow-Up Investigation: _____

_____

_____

Source #4: _____
　　　　　　　　　　　Title　　　　　　　　　　　　　　　Author　　　　　　　　　Date

Synopsis of my findings: _____

_____

_____

_____

_____

_____

_____

_____

Issues for Follow-Up Investigation: _____

_____

_____

PLAN OF ACTION

Use the knowledge you have gained from your research to develop and implement
a Plan of Action that will take your project to a high level of success.

(Use additional paper if necessary.)

Plan of Action: _____

_____

_____

_____

_____

_____

_____

_____

_____

The Service-Learning Project will achieve the following objectives and/or have the

following attributes: _____

_____

_____

_____

_____

_____

_____

JOURNAL FOR WEEK #1 / PROJECT #1

Goal for Week #1: _____
_____
_____
_____

Action Taken: _____
_____
_____
_____
_____
_____

Principal Challenges: _____
_____
_____
_____
_____
_____

Principal Success: _____
_____
_____
_____

Plan for Week #2: _____
_____
_____
_____

PROGRESS CHART FOR WEEK #1 / PROJECT #1

- ❖ Take a moment to reflect on the statements below.
- ❖ Fill in the bar charts to document where you are in regard to the statements.
- ❖ Provide a title for the final two bar charts that describes an area that you want to develop.
- ❖ The goal is to rise to 100%.

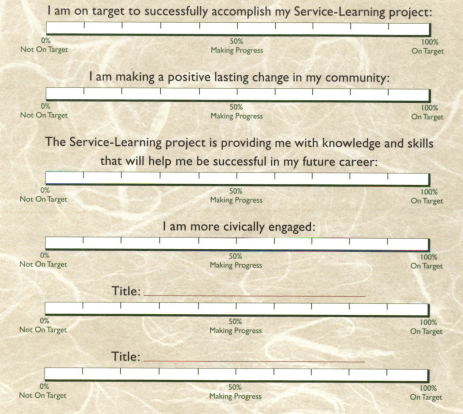

I am on target to successfully accomplish my Service-Learning project:

0% — Not On Target 50% — Making Progress 100% — On Target

I am making a positive lasting change in my community:

0% — Not On Target 50% — Making Progress 100% — On Target

The Service-Learning project is providing me with knowledge and skills that will help me be successful in my future career:

0% — Not On Target 50% — Making Progress 100% — On Target

I am more civically engaged:

0% — Not On Target 50% — Making Progress 100% — On Target

Title: _____

0% — Not On Target 50% — Making Progress 100% — On Target

Title: _____

0% — Not On Target 50% — Making Progress 100% — On Target

I commit to taking the following action to achieve 100% in regard to the above statements:

_____

_____

_____

_____

_____

JOURNAL FOR WEEK #2 / PROJECT #2

Goal for Week #2: _____
_____
_____
_____

Action Taken: _____
_____
_____
_____
_____
_____

Principal Challenges: _____
_____
_____
_____
_____
_____

Principal Success: _____
_____
_____
_____

Plan for Week #3: _____
_____
_____
_____

◆ Take a moment to reflect on the statements below.

◆ Fill in the bar charts to document where you are in regard to the statements.

◆ Provide a title for the final two bar charts that describes an area that you want to develop.

◆ The goal is to rise to 100%.

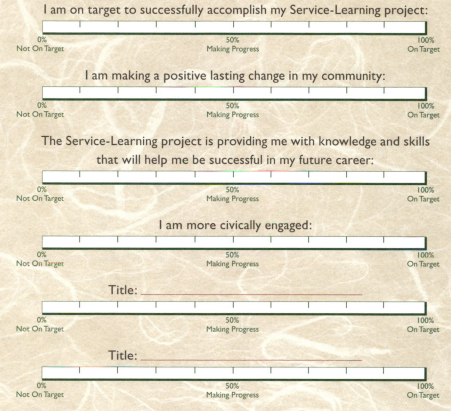

I am on target to successfully accomplish my Service-Learning project:

0% — 50% — 100%
Not On Target — Making Progress — On Target

I am making a positive lasting change in my community:

0% — 50% — 100%
Not On Target — Making Progress — On Target

The Service-Learning project is providing me with knowledge and skills that will help me be successful in my future career:

0% — 50% — 100%
Not On Target — Making Progress — On Target

I am more civically engaged:

0% — 50% — 100%
Not On Target — Making Progress — On Target

Title: _____

0% — 50% — 100%
Not On Target — Making Progress — On Target

Title: _____

0% — 50% — 100%
Not On Target — Making Progress — On Target

I commit to taking the following action to achieve 100% in regard to the above statements:

_____

_____

_____

_____

JOURNAL FOR WEEK #3 / PROJECT #3

Goal for Week #3: _____
_____
_____
_____

Action Taken: _____
_____
_____
_____
_____
_____
_____

Principal Challenges: _____
_____
_____
_____
_____
_____

Principal Success: _____
_____
_____
_____

Plan for Week #4: _____
_____
_____
_____

PROGRESS CHART FOR WEEK #3 / PROJECT #3

- ❖ Take a moment to reflect on the statements below.
- ❖ Fill in the bar charts to document where you are in regard to the statements.
- ❖ Provide a title for the final two bar charts that describes an area that you want to develop.
- ❖ The goal is to rise to 100%.

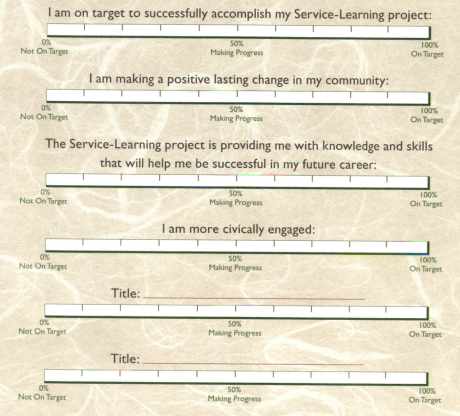

I am on target to successfully accomplish my Service-Learning project:

0%   50%   100%
Not On Target   Making Progress   On Target

I am making a positive lasting change in my community:

0%   50%   100%
Not On Target   Making Progress   On Target

The Service-Learning project is providing me with knowledge and skills
that will help me be successful in my future career:

0%   50%   100%
Not On Target   Making Progress   On Target

I am more civically engaged:

0%   50%   100%
Not On Target   Making Progress   On Target

Title: _____

0%   50%   100%
Not On Target   Making Progress   On Target

Title: _____

0%   50%   100%
Not On Target   Making Progress   On Target

I commit to taking the following action to achieve 100% in regard to the above statements:

_____

_____

_____

_____

_____

JOURNAL FOR WEEK #4 / PROJECT #4

Goal for Week #4: _____
_____
_____
_____

Action Taken: _____
_____
_____
_____
_____
_____

Principal Challenges: _____
_____
_____
_____
_____
_____
_____

Principal Success: _____
_____
_____
_____

Plan for Week #5: _____
_____
_____
_____

PROGRESS CHART FOR WEEK #4 / PROJECT #4

- Take a moment to reflect on the statements below.
- Fill in the bar charts to document where you are in regard to the statements.
- Provide a title for the final two bar charts that describes an area that you want to develop.
- The goal is to rise to 100%.

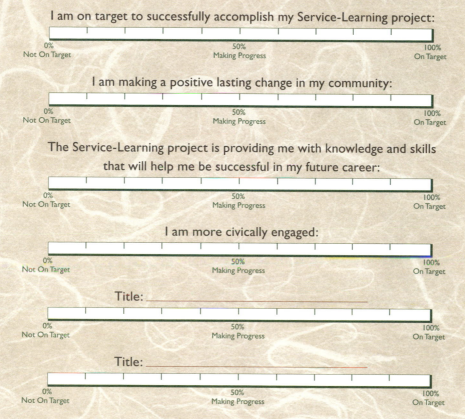

I am on target to successfully accomplish my Service-Learning project:

0% — Not On Target 50% — Making Progress 100% — On Target

I am making a positive lasting change in my community:

0% — Not On Target 50% — Making Progress 100% — On Target

The Service-Learning project is providing me with knowledge and skills that will help me be successful in my future career:

0% — Not On Target 50% — Making Progress 100% — On Target

I am more civically engaged:

0% — Not On Target 50% — Making Progress 100% — On Target

Title: _____

0% — Not On Target 50% — Making Progress 100% — On Target

Title: _____

0% — Not On Target 50% — Making Progress 100% — On Target

I commit to taking the following action to achieve 100% in regard to the above statements:

_____

_____

_____

_____

_____

Goal for Week #5: _____
_____
_____
_____

Action Taken: _____
_____
_____
_____
_____

Principal Challenges: _____
_____
_____
_____
_____
_____

Principal Success: _____
_____
_____
_____

Plan for Week #6: _____
_____
_____
_____

PROGRESS CHART FOR WEEK #5 / PROJECT #5

- Take a moment to reflect on the statements below.
- Fill in the bar charts to document where you are in regard to the statements.
- Provide a title for the final two bar charts that describes an area that you want to develop.
- The goal is to rise to 100%.

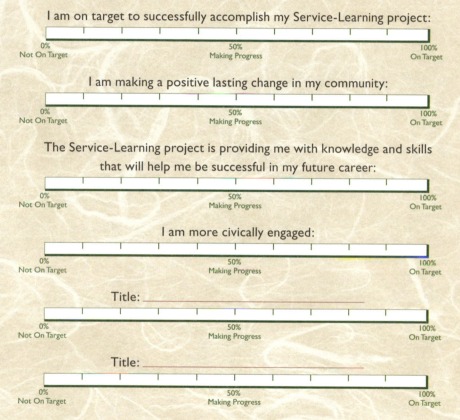

I am on target to successfully accomplish my Service-Learning project:

0% — Not On Target   50% — Making Progress   100% — On Target

I am making a positive lasting change in my community:

0% — Not On Target   50% — Making Progress   100% — On Target

The Service-Learning project is providing me with knowledge and skills that will help me be successful in my future career:

0% — Not On Target   50% — Making Progress   100% — On Target

I am more civically engaged:

0% — Not On Target   50% — Making Progress   100% — On Target

Title: _____

0% — Not On Target   50% — Making Progress   100% — On Target

Title: _____

0% — Not On Target   50% — Making Progress   100% — On Target

I commit to taking the following action to achieve 100% in regard to the above statements:

_____

_____

_____

_____

JOURNAL FOR WEEK #6 / PROJECT #6

Goal for Week #6: _____
_____
_____
_____

Action Taken: _____
_____
_____
_____
_____
_____
_____

Principal Challenges: _____
_____
_____
_____
_____
_____
_____

Principal Success: _____
_____
_____
_____

Plan for Week #7: _____
_____
_____
_____

PROGRESS CHART FOR WEEK #6 / PROJECT #6

- ❖ Take a moment to reflect on the statements below.
- ❖ Fill in the bar charts to document where you are in regard to the statements.
- ❖ Provide a title for the final two bar charts that describes an area that you want to develop.
- ❖ The goal is to rise to 100%.

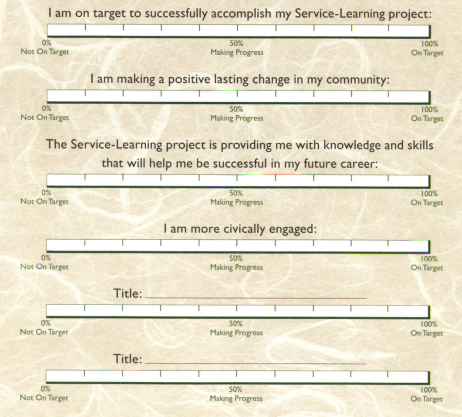

I am on target to successfully accomplish my Service-Learning project:

0% — Not On Target   50% — Making Progress   100% — On Target

I am making a positive lasting change in my community:

0% — Not On Target   50% — Making Progress   100% — On Target

The Service-Learning project is providing me with knowledge and skills that will help me be successful in my future career:

0% — Not On Target   50% — Making Progress   100% — On Target

I am more civically engaged:

0% — Not On Target   50% — Making Progress   100% — On Target

Title: _____

0% — Not On Target   50% — Making Progress   100% — On Target

Title: _____

0% — Not On Target   50% — Making Progress   100% — On Target

I commit to taking the following action to achieve 100% in regard to the above statements:

_____

_____

_____

_____

_____

JOURNAL FOR WEEK #7 / PROJECT #7

Goal for Week #7: _____
_____
_____
_____

Action Taken: _____
_____
_____
_____
_____
_____
_____

Principal Challenges: _____
_____
_____
_____
_____
_____

Principal Success: _____
_____
_____
_____

Plan for Week #8: _____
_____
_____
_____

- ❖ Take a moment to reflect on the statements below.
- ❖ Fill in the bar charts to document where you are in regard to the statements.
- ❖ Provide a title for the final two bar charts that describes an area that you want to develop.
- ❖ The goal is to rise to 100%.

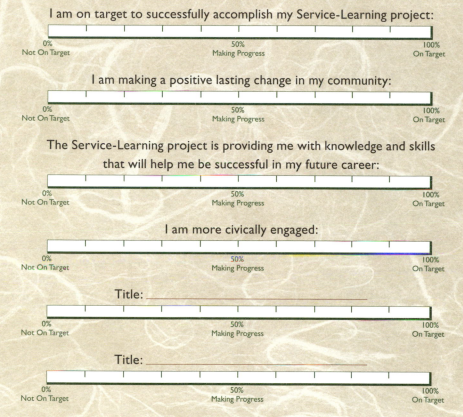

I am on target to successfully accomplish my Service-Learning project:

| 0% | 50% | 100% |
| Not On Target | Making Progress | On Target |

I am making a positive lasting change in my community:

| 0% | 50% | 100% |
| Not On Target | Making Progress | On Target |

The Service-Learning project is providing me with knowledge and skills
that will help me be successful in my future career:

| 0% | 50% | 100% |
| Not On Target | Making Progress | On Target |

I am more civically engaged:

| 0% | 50% | 100% |
| Not On Target | Making Progress | On Target |

Title: _____

| 0% | 50% | 100% |
| Not On Target | Making Progress | On Target |

Title: _____

| 0% | 50% | 100% |
| Not On Target | Making Progress | On Target |

I commit to taking the following action to achieve 100% in regard to the above statements:

_____

_____

_____

_____

_____

JOURNAL FOR WEEK #8 / PROJECT #8

Goal for Week #8: _____

_____

_____

_____

Action Taken: _____

_____

_____

_____

_____

_____

Principal Challenges: _____

_____

_____

_____

_____

_____

Principal Success: _____

_____

_____

_____

Plan for Week #9: _____

_____

_____

_____

❖ Take a moment to reflect on the statements below.

❖ Fill in the bar charts to document where you are in regard to the statements.

❖ Provide a title for the final two bar charts that describes an area that you want to develop.

❖ The goal is to rise to 100%.

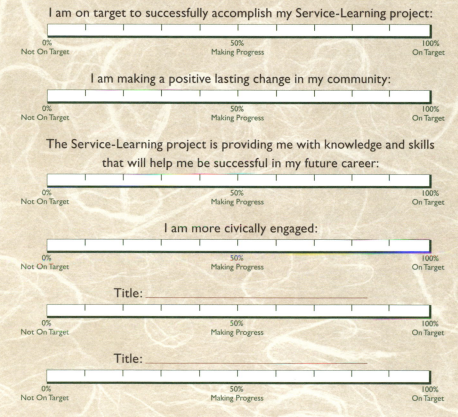

I am on target to successfully accomplish my Service-Learning project:

0%
Not On Target

50%
Making Progress

100%
On Target

I am making a positive lasting change in my community:

0%
Not On Target

50%
Making Progress

100%
On Target

The Service-Learning project is providing me with knowledge and skills that will help me be successful in my future career:

0%
Not On Target

50%
Making Progress

100%
On Target

I am more civically engaged:

0%
Not On Target

50%
Making Progress

100%
On Target

Title: _____

0%
Not On Target

50%
Making Progress

100%
On Target

Title: _____

0%
Not On Target

50%
Making Progress

100%
On Target

I commit to taking the following action to achieve 100% in regard to the above statements:

_____

_____

_____

_____

_____

JOURNAL FOR WEEK #9 / PROJECT #9

Goal for Week #9: _____

_____

_____

_____

Action Taken: _____

_____

_____

_____

_____

_____

Principal Challenges: _____

_____

_____

_____

_____

_____

Principal Success: _____

_____

_____

_____

Plan for Week #10: _____

_____

_____

_____

◆ Take a moment to reflect on the statements below.
◆ Fill in the bar charts to document where you are in regard to the statements.
◆ Provide a title for the final two bar charts that describes an area that you want to develop.
◆ The goal is to rise to 100%.

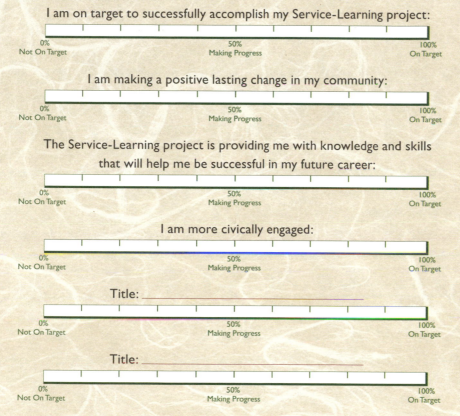

I am on target to successfully accomplish my Service-Learning project:

0%   50%   100%
Not On Target   Making Progress   On Target

I am making a positive lasting change in my community:

0%   50%   100%
Not On Target   Making Progress   On Target

The Service-Learning project is providing me with knowledge and skills that will help me be successful in my future career:

0%   50%   100%
Not On Target   Making Progress   On Target

I am more civically engaged:

0%   50%   100%
Not On Target   Making Progress   On Target

Title: _____

0%   50%   100%
Not On Target   Making Progress   On Target

Title: _____

0%   50%   100%
Not On Target   Making Progress   On Target

I commit to taking the following action to achieve 100% in regard to the above statements:

_____

_____

_____

_____

_____

JOURNAL FOR WEEK #10 / PROJECT #10

Goal for Week #10: _____
_____
_____
_____

Action Taken: _____
_____
_____
_____
_____
_____

Principal Challenges: _____
_____
_____
_____
_____
_____

Principal Success: _____
_____
_____
_____
_____
_____
_____

SERVICE-LEARNING
STUDENT'S GUIDE & JOURNAL

Helping You Take Service-Learning to a Higher Level of Achievement Through Building Personal Character – Scholastic Achievement Developing Leaders – Service to the Community

The **Service-Learning - Student's Guide & Journal** will help you to easily bring high quality Service-Learning into your school. This is a complete Service-Learning program, in addition to the books you will

The **Service-Learning – Student's Guide & Journal** will help your students:

➤ Organize, document, and guide their Service-Learning project
➤ Improve their thinking and writing skills
➤ Develop personal character and scholastic achievement
➤ Expand civic awareness
➤ Take action to improve the lives of others in the community

Thousands of students from all fifty states, K-12 and Higher Education, are using these books to take their service to their community and the nation to a higher level of success. Instructors are delighted with the results. For example, Emily Lopez, Service-Learning director from New York, comments that: *"The **Service Learning Journals** are great! The journals provided direction for our students and the students were able to see their progress. As for the service providers (the teachers and case managers), they were able to track and assess the academic and social growth of their students. A very valuable tool for the educational development for our youth!"*

I look forward to speaking with you soon.

Best Regards,
Robert Schoenfeld

PS: You will find ordering information on the back of this page. You may view pages from the books at: www.ServiceLearn.com

5235 S. Graham St. Seattle, WA 98118 • Tel: 206-722-1988 • Fax: 206-721-3200
Email: Info@ServiceLearn.com • Website: www.ServiceLearn.com

❖ Take a moment to reflect on the statements below.

❖ Fill in the bar charts to document where you are in regard to the statements.

❖ Provide a title for the final two bar charts that describes an area that you want to develop.

❖ The goal is to rise to 100%.

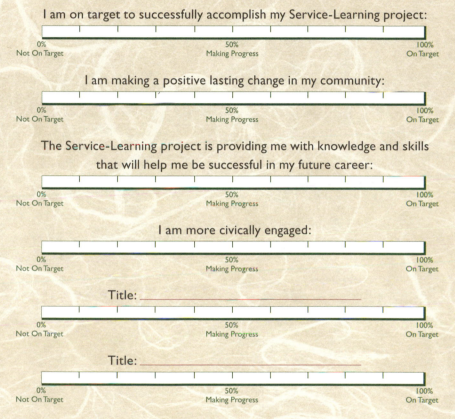

I am on target to successfully accomplish my Service-Learning project:

0% — Not On Target   50% — Making Progress   100% — On Target

I am making a positive lasting change in my community:

0% — Not On Target   50% — Making Progress   100% — On Target

The Service-Learning project is providing me with knowledge and skills that will help me be successful in my future career:

0% — Not On Target   50% — Making Progress   100% — On Target

I am more civically engaged:

0% — Not On Target   50% — Making Progress   100% — On Target

Title: _____

0% — Not On Target   50% — Making Progress   100% — On Target

Title: _____

0% — Not On Target   50% — Making Progress   100% — On Target

I commit to taking the following action to achieve 100% in regard to the above statements:

_____

_____

_____

_____

_____

TIME LINE RECORD

Record Your Service-Learning Participation
(Supervisor's signature may not be required — check with the instructor)

Date	Hours	Summary	Supervisor Signature

TIME LINE RECORD

Date	Hours	Summary	Supervisor Signature

VISION FOR MY FUTURE

Here is what I want to accomplish this year:

Education: _____

_____

_____

_____

Career: _____

_____

_____

_____

Family and Friends: _____

_____

_____

_____

Involvement and Service to My Community: _____

_____

_____

_____

Personal Growth: _____

_____

_____

_____

Other: _____

_____

_____

_____

VISION FOR MY FUTURE

Here is what I want to accomplish in the next 5 years:

Education: _____
_____
_____
_____

Career: _____
_____
_____
_____

Family and Friends: _____
_____
_____
_____

Involvement and Service to My Community: _____
_____
_____
_____

Personal Growth: _____
_____
_____
_____

Other: _____
_____
_____
_____

VISION FOR MY FUTURE

Here is what I want to accomplish in the next 20 years:

Education: _____

_____

_____

_____

Career: _____

_____

_____

_____

Family and Friends: _____

_____

_____

_____

Involvement and Service to My Community: _____

_____

_____

_____

Personal Growth: _____

_____

_____

_____

Other: _____

_____

_____

_____

JOURNAL

Record your thoughts, reflections, ideas, and observations.
Reviewing your journal entries throughout the Service-Learning
project will help you fine-tune your actions.
Your Journal entries will also be useful in the final presentation.
(Please date your Journal entries – use additional paper as needed)

REFLECTIONS

Here are the Knowledge and Skills that I have acquired as a direct result of taking part in this Service-Learning project:

_____

_____

_____

_____

_____

_____

_____

_____

Here is how this Service-Learning project ties in with my

_____ **class:**

(Course Title)

_____

_____

_____

_____

_____

_____

_____

My Contribution to the Community

I have devoted _____ hours to my Service-Learning project.
Here are four lasting positive changes to the community that
are an outcome of my Service-Learning project:

1 _____
_____
_____
_____

2 _____
_____
_____
_____

3 _____
_____
_____
_____

4 _____
_____
_____
_____

CULMINATION

Presentation

At the conclusion of the class, you will give a presentation to demonstrate that you have fulfilled the course objectives. The presentation will include the Service-Learning project's mission, what you have learned from being involved in the project, how the project ties in with your class studies, the ways you have contributed to making your community better, and your thoughts and reflections about your involvement in the project. Be creative — the presentation can be a video, PowerPoint, multimedia, or a formal paper.

Congratulations

Congratulations. You have made an important improvement to your community and acquired useful knowledge and skills along the way.

Thank You for Your Service

Keep in mind, there is more to be done and this is only the beginning. Talk with your friends, professors, and mentors and start brainstorming and/or planning your next venture in service to your community, the nation, and the world.

Planning My Next Service-Learning Project

Topics and Issues I Want to Explore:

_____

_____

_____

_____

_____

_____

_____

INSTRUCTOR'S COMMENTS & EVALUATION

CONTACTS

Instructor's Name: _____

Email: _____ Phone Number: _____

Community Service Provider's Name: _____

Email: _____ Phone Number: _____

Mentor's Name: _____

Email: _____ Phone Number: _____

Mentee's Name: _____

Email: _____ Phone Number: _____

Name: _____

Email: _____ Phone Number: _____

Name: _____

Email: _____ Phone Number: _____

Name: _____

Email: _____ Phone Number: _____

Name: _____

Email: _____ Phone Number: _____

Name: _____

Email: _____ Phone Number: _____

REFERENCE WEBSITES

www._____ www._____

www._____ www._____

www._____ www._____